Pitsy is Missing!

Written by

Mosina Jordan

Illustrated by Valerie Bouthyette

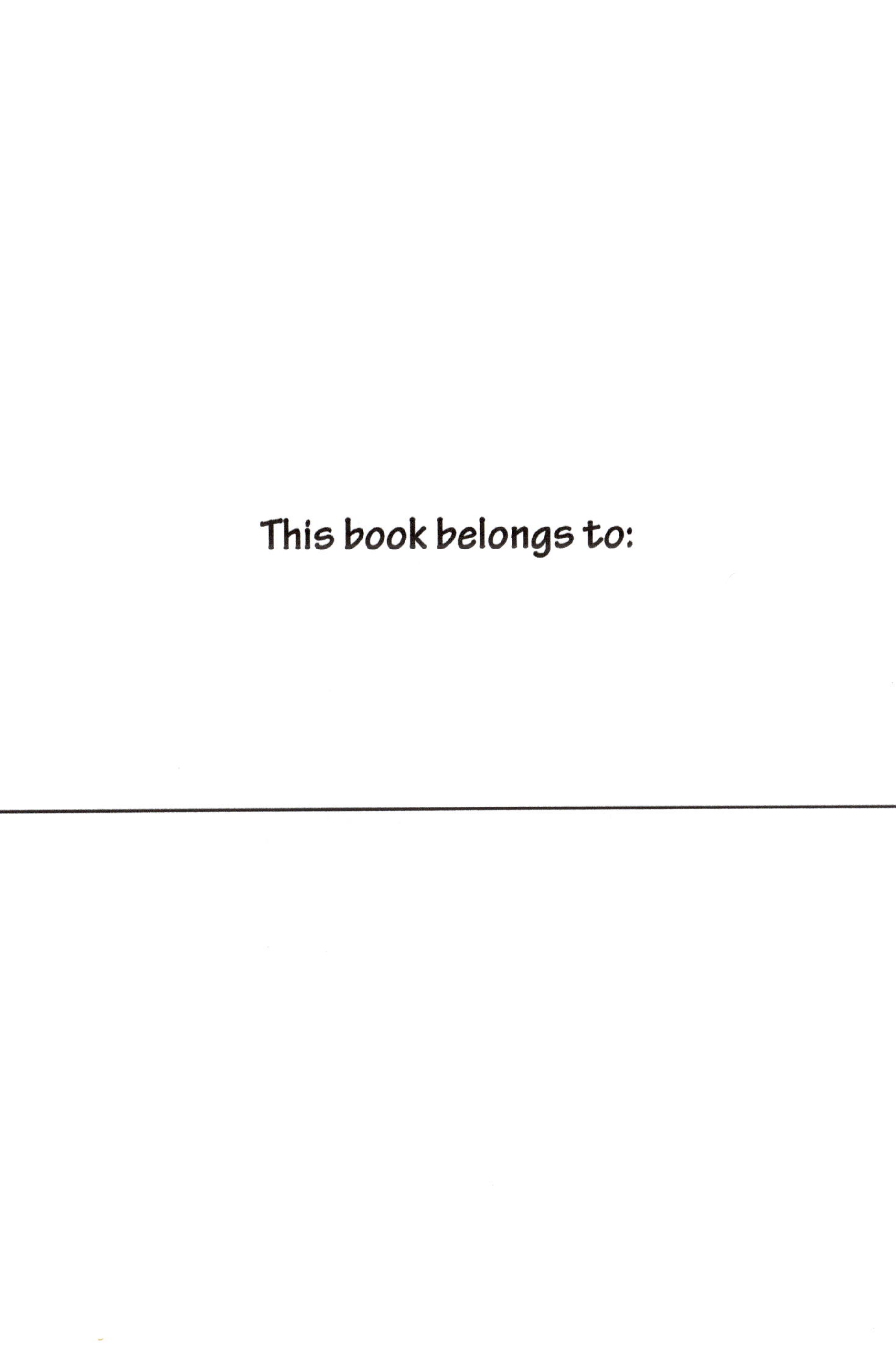

This book belongs to:

____

My name is Michele. We've just moved into
a new neighborhood and a wonderful house.
I love my new school which is only five blocks
from where we live. My brothers, Frank and Michael
had pets, a hamster and two birds - finches.
I was very unhappy that I didn't have a pet.
Mom promised me that we would go to the animal
shelter and select an animal of my choice
on Saturday. Today was Monday and I had to
wait five days until Saturday.
I wasn't sure I could wait that long.

Frank named his hamster, Jogger.
I think he named him Jogger because he ran on
the wheel in his cage all day. He never seemed to
get tired. He only stopped to eat,
drink water and sleep at night.

Frank was responsible for feeding
Jogger and keeping his cage clean. He also had to
buy the food for the hamster out his weekly
allowance and money he had saved from
birthday and Christmas gifts. Mom would help
him out when he didn't have enough money.

Jogger lived in the basement and after school
we would visit with him. I don't know if he knew we
were there since he was so busy running all the time.

Michael also had to feed the finches, clean their
cage and buy their food. Michael named the birds
Jack and Jill because they were male and female.

Michael kept the birds in a cage on the
screened-in back porch. The birds could see
the backyard, daylight, trees, flowers, squirrels,
other birds, the moon and the stars.
We also checked-in on Jack and Jill
after school each day.

The week was going by so-ooo slowly -
Tuesday, Wednesday, Thursday and Friday.
All I could think about in school all week was
going to the animal shelter.

Finally, Saturday was here. Mom, Michael, Frank
and I went to the animal shelter. I was surprised
to see so many animals.

Mom said, if I select a dog,
I will need to walk him in the morning before school,
in the afternoon after school and before I go to bed.
She said that dogs and cats are like family members
and require special treatment.

ANIMAL SHELTER

I walked up and down the aisles of the shelter
looking for just the right pet. And, there she was
a cat with white paws and dark gray and white fur.
As I passed the cage, the cat came to the front of
the cage to say hello and I knew she was the one.
And, in fact, she was a female cat.

Just what I wanted. My Mom adopted the cat
and before we could get into the car,
I gave the cat a name, Pitsy.

On the way home, we stopped by a pet store
to buy what we needed to care for Pitsy, a litter box,
litter, cat food, a bowl and a bed.
I owed Mom a lot money for Pitsy's supplies.
There went my savings and allowances!

I took Pitsy to my room on the second floor
and set-up her bed. She walked around my room
and seemed to like it.

We then went to the basement where I put the litterbox
and filled it with litter. She knew just what to do
and used it right away.

Next, to the kitchen, where I placed her bowl and fed her.
Pitsy walked around the house checking everything out.

She seemed to like her new
home. I spent most of the
day petting Pitsy
while she purred.
Purring means
she is happy and content.

Pitsy enjoyed her new home and everyone
enjoyed having Pitsy around. It wasn't difficult
taking care of Pitsy, changing the litter in her litterbox,
feeding her and loving her. For over a year, Pitsy didn't
go outside of the house. She seemed content to
explore all the nooks and crannies in the house.

Checking-on Jogger in the basement,
I'm sure she thought he must be tired
running all the time.

When she was on the back porch,
I'm sure she looked at Jack and Jill,
wondering how she could get into the
cage and eat them.
They were lucky she couldn't get into the cage.

Every day, when I came home from school,
before doing my homework,
I spent an hour playing with Pitsy.

One day, when I came home from school,
I couldn't find Pitsy.
Michael and Frank helped me look everywhere for her.
It was clear, she wasn't in the house.

Pitsy is missing!

I asked Mom if she would help us look In the
neighborhood for Pitsy.

I had no idea where she would go.

We walked up and down all the streets
surrounding our house, calling Pitsy's name.
She was nowhere to be found.

Mom said, "Don't worry, she'll come home.
She is probably exploring the neighborhood
and making new friends.
When she is hungry, she'll come home."

I was so upset, I started crying.
Michael, Frank and I went home with Mom.
We worked on our homework
and then sat down for dinner.
Pitsy still hadn't returned and I was so sad
and worried, I could hardly eat dinner.

I took my bath and said a prayer for
Pitsy before going to sleep.

In the morning, I got up early,
woke-up Michael and Frank
and told them to get dressed; that I needed them
to help me look for Pitsy on the way to school.

After breakfast, we were off and we still didn't
see her anywhere. I couldn't concentrate on my
school work, wondering where Pitsy could be and what
she was doing. I was thinking she should be hungry
by now. When school was out, Michael, Frank and I looked
for Pitsy on the way home, walking a couple of blocks out
of the way to search for her.

When we arrived home, I was very sad.
I couldn't concentrate on my homework,
so I visited with Jogger and Jack and Jill and ate a
snack. I walked around the block by myself calling
Pitsy's name, but couldn't find her. I came home and
did my homework. As I finished my homework,
it was time for dinner.

Just as we were finishing dinner,
we heard Pitsy meowing at the back-porch door.
I let Pitsy in and she ran to the kitchen
and sat down by her bowl.

I couldn't believe it! Mom was right, Pitsy came
home when she was hungry. She knew where she lived!

I fed her and finished my dinner. Since it was late,
I didn't have much time to spend with Pitsy before going
to bed. By the time I got into bed, Pitsy was already
in her bed and fast asleep.
I guess she had a great adventure.

I worried about how she got out of the house.
But, after thinking about it,
I realized that Pitsy knew where her home was.
She would never be lost.